Superfast
ROCKETS

by Donna Latham
Consultant: Michelle Nichols, Master Educator
Adler Planetarium & Astronomy Museum
Chicago, Illinois

BEARPORT
PUBLISHING COMPANY, INC.
New York, New York

Credits

Cover, NASA (National Aeronautics and Space Administration); Title Page, NASA (National Aeronautics and Space Administration); 4, NASA (National Aeronautics and Space Administration); 5, NASA (National Aeronautics and Space Administration); 6, NASA (National Aeronautics and Space Administration); 7, Steve Stankiewitz; 8, Courtesy of Artist Charles Hubble/TRW Inc. and Western Reserve History Society/NASA; 9, NASA (National Aeronautics and Space Administration); 10(L), Bettmann/Corbis; 10(R) TASS/Sovfoto; 11, Corbis; 12, Topham-HIP/The Image Works; 13, AP Wide World Photos; 14, Bettmann/Corbis; 15(L), AP Wide World Photos; 15(R) Bettmann/Corbis; 16, NASA (National Aeronautics and Space Administration); 17, TASS/Sovfoto; 18, NASA (National Aeronautics and Space Administration); 19, NASA (National Aeronautics and Space Administration); 20, NASA (National Aeronautics and Space Administration); 21, NASA (National Aeronautics and Space Administration); 22, Courtesy of David Weeks; 23, Sven Knudson; 24, NASA (National Aeronautics and Space Administration); 25, AP Wide World Photos; 26(L), Bettmann/Corbis; 26(R), NASA (National Aeronautics and Space Administration); 27, NASA (National Aeronautics and Space Administration)/Photo Researchers, Inc.; 29, NASA (National Aeronautics and Space Administration).

Editorial development by Judy Nayer
Design & Production by Paula Jo Smith

Library of Congress Cataloging-in-Publication Data

Latham, Donna.
  Superfast rockets / by Donna Latham.
      p. cm.—(Ultimate speed)
  Includes bibliographical references and index.
  ISBN 1-59716-083-0 (library binding)—ISBN 1-59716-120-9 (pbk.)
 1. Rocketry—History—Juvenile literature. 2. Rockets (Aeronautics)—History—Juvenile literature.
I. Title: Super fast rockets. II. Title. III. Series.

  TL782.5.L37 2006
  621.43'56—dc22

                    2005006602

For more information, write to Bearport Publishing Company, Inc., 101 Fifth Avenue, Suite 6R, New York, New York 10003. Printed in the United States of America.

1 2 3 4 5 6 7 8 9 10

CONTENTS

Perched on a Bomb

Inside the cramped **capsule**, astronaut John Glenn waited. The *Friendship 7* launch was running late. When the crew had squeezed John into the tiny capsule, they broke a bolt on the **hatch**. They scrambled to replace it. Now, with a new bolt in place, the countdown could finally begin.

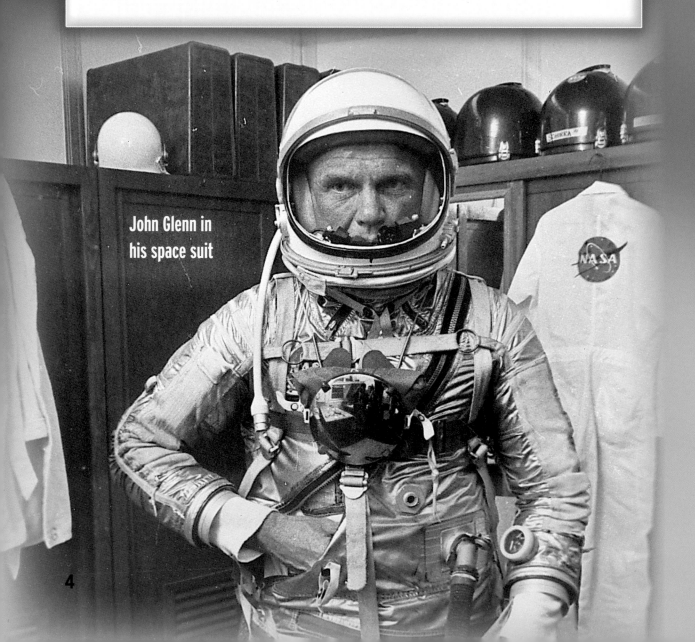

John Glenn in his space suit

It was February 20, 1962. Spaceflight was in its early stages. In his silver suit, John sat at the controls. His capsule rested on top of a rocket. With explosive **fuel** beneath him, John was perched on a bomb. He was risking his life to become the first American to **orbit** Earth.

Because of cramped capsules, early astronauts could be no taller than 5' 11''. At just over 5' 10'', John Glenn was a tight fit!

John Glenn squeezes into *Friendship 7*'s capsule.

How Does a Rocket Work?

By the 1960s, rockets were finally powerful enough to blast out of Earth's **gravity**. To gain speed quickly, however, they had to burn lots of fuel. Gases from the burning fuel shot out behind the rockets and pushed them into space.

Gases roar out the back of the rocket.

Fuels need **oxygen** to burn. Since there is no air in space, rockets must carry their own oxygen supplies.

Rockets are built in stages, or sections. Each part holds its own fuel. After a stage burns all its fuel, it drops away. Now the rocket weighs less. Then, the next stage fires up. The less weight the rocket carries, the faster it shoots through space.

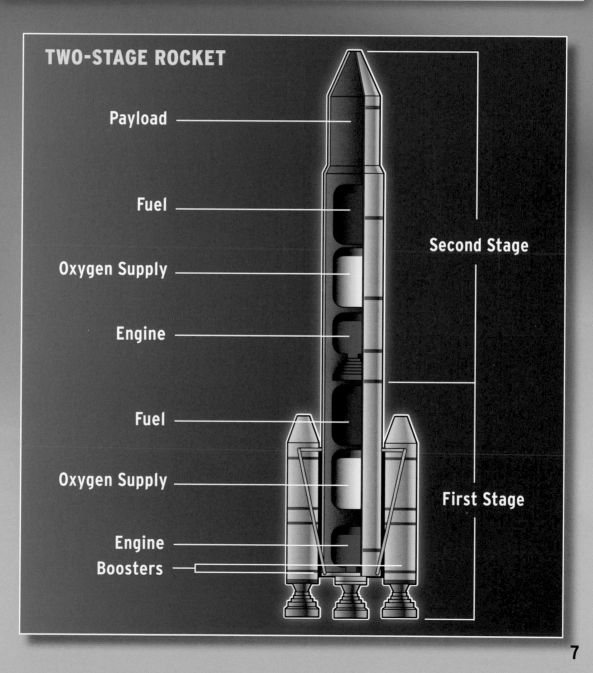

TWO-STAGE ROCKET

Payload

Fuel

Oxygen Supply

Engine

Second Stage

Fuel

Oxygen Supply

Engine

Boosters

First Stage

Fire Arrows and the First Step Rocket

Though very different from *Friendship 7*, rockets have been around for many years. The Chinese launched the first rockets in 1232. They were called "fire arrows." These early rockets were bamboo tubes stuffed with gunpowder. They were used in wars and for fireworks.

Gunpowder, an exploding solid fuel, powered fire arrows.

Later, people in Europe and the Middle East also began making rockets. By 1591, Germany's Johann Schmidlap (YO-hahn SHMID-lahp) built the first "step rocket." It had two stages—a small rocket on top of a larger one. When the larger rocket ran out of fuel, it fell away. The smaller rocket then fired up and blasted to greater heights.

Rocket boosters attached to the space shuttle provide extra power during liftoff. Then, the boosters fall away.

Schmidlap's ideas paved the way for today's staged rockets.

Liquid-Fuel Rockets

In 1903, Konstantin Tsiolkovsky (KUN-stun-tyeen TSEE-ohl-KOVE-skee), a Russian teacher, wrote an important paper. He suggested that liquid-fuel rockets be used for spaceflight. Unlike solid gunpowder, liquid fuels could lift rockets out of Earth's **atmosphere**.

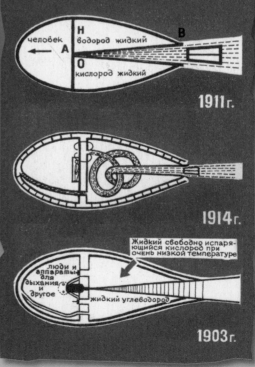

Tsiolkovsky's liquid-fuel rocket designs

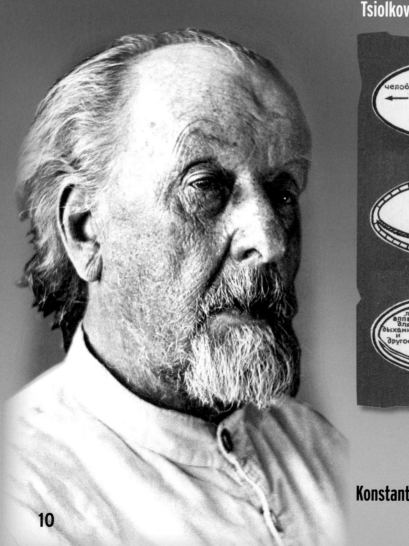

Konstantin Tsiolkovsky

In 1926, Robert Goddard (GAHD-durd), an American scientist, fired the first liquid-fuel rocket. He shot it from his aunt Effie's farm. Its quick flight lasted only seconds. Filled with gasoline and liquid oxygen, the rocket **soared** 40 feet (12 m) before landing in a cabbage patch! At 60 miles per hour (97 kph), the rocket was hardly superfast. However, Goddard's liquid-fuel rocket paved the way for *Friendship 7*.

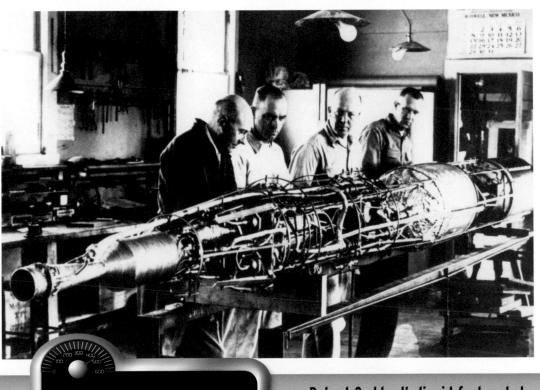

Goddard's rocket flew at a speed easily reached by today's cars.

Robert Goddard's liquid-fuel rocket

V-2 War Rockets

In the 1930s, Germany built the V-2—the first long-range rocket. V-2s were weapons that could bomb faraway places. In 1942, during World War II, Germany showered thousands of V-2s on England.

Used as weapons, the fierce V-2 rockets wiped out entire sections of London, England.

That same year, John Glenn trained to become a Marine Corps pilot. As the war went on, he flew as a fighter pilot.

After Germany's fall in 1945, many of its scientists moved to either the United States or the Soviet Union. In the United States, German scientist Wernher von Braun (VAIR-nuhr VAHN BROWN) led a team that built rockets for space travel. The space race was on!

Wernher von Braun

In Germany, von Braun had helped create the V-2. It traveled at the ferocious speed of 3,500 miles per hour (5,633 kph).

Sputnik and Space Creatures

The space age began on October 4, 1957, when the Soviet **spacecraft** *Sputnik* (SPOOHT-nihk) was launched into space. It was the first man-made **satellite** to orbit Earth. *Sputnik* was only the size of a basketball. Yet, it made huge changes in the world.

Sputnik traveled at the superfast speed of 17,500 miles per hour (28,164 kph), five times the speed of V-2 rockets.

Sputnik, which weighed less than 200 pounds (91 kg), stayed in orbit for three months. Then, it fell back to Earth.

The United States and the Soviet Union both wanted to lead the race into space. When *Sputnik* was launched, the Americans were afraid they were falling behind in the race. They reacted quickly. About a year after *Sputnik* went into orbit, the United States formed an organization dedicated to space exploration—the National Aeronautics and Space Administration (NASA).

A month after *Sputnik's* launch, the Soviets blasted the first living thing into space, a dog named Laika (LIE-kuh).

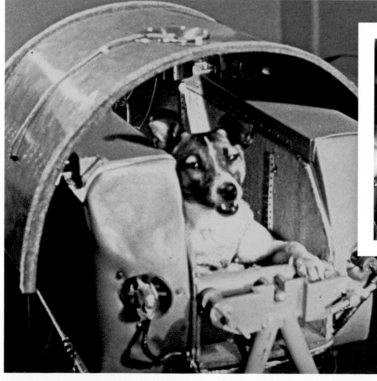

Later, in 1960, the Soviets sent two more dogs into space—Strelka and Belka.

The Mercury Seven

On April 9, 1959, NASA introduced the Mercury Seven—the first astronauts. This group of brave men included war hero John Glenn.

The purpose of NASA's Mercury program was to send a man into orbit. Then, scientists on Earth could study a human's reaction to space travel.

The Mercury Seven: (*back row, from left*) Alan B. Shepard, Jr., Virgil I. "Gus" Grissom, L. Gordon Cooper, Jr.; (*front row, from left*) Walter M. Schirra, Jr., Donald K. "Deke" Slayton, John H. Glenn, Jr., M. Scott Carpenter

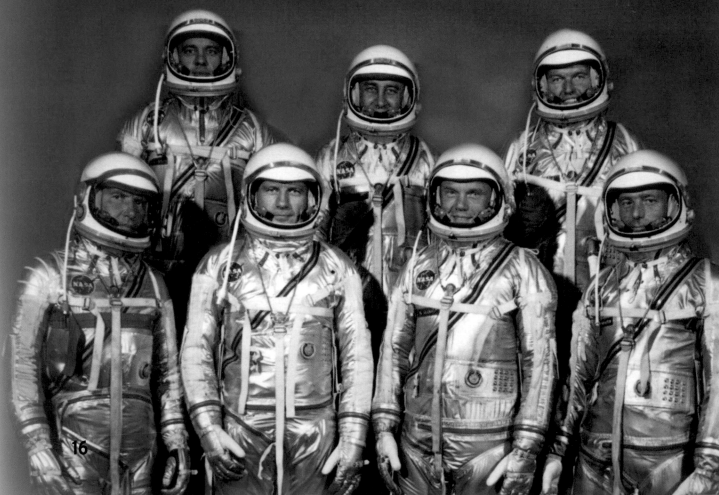

As John and the others trained, many Americans followed their progress. Who would be the first person to ride a rocket into space? On April 12, 1961, everyone found out. It was not one of the Mercury Seven. Instead, the first person in space was Soviet **cosmonaut** Yuri Gagarin (YOOR-ee Gah-GAHR-ihn).

Gagarin spent almost two hours in space as he orbited Earth.

In space, Gagarin scribbled notes about his flight—until his pencil floated away.

"Godspeed, John Glenn"

Again, the United States reacted quickly. On May 5, 1961, Alan B. Shepard became the first American in space. Virgil "Gus" Grissom followed on July 21, 1961. Redstone rockets hurled each of the astronauts high above Earth. However, they were not strong enough to blast the men into orbit.

Alan B. Shepard is hoisted up after landing at sea.

Next it was John Glenn's turn to make history. Sitting in *Friendship 7*, an Atlas rocket, John heard Scott Carpenter's voice over the radio.

"**Godspeed**, John Glenn," Carpenter called. In seconds, the rocket thundered off. Soaring higher into space, it zoomed faster and faster. It quickly hit the superfast speed needed for orbit.

John Glenn's flight using an Atlas rocket was risky. Earlier Atlas rockets had exploded.

It took just five minutes for *Friendship 7* to reach its orbital speed of 17,500 miles per hour (28,164 kph).

Trouble at Superfast Speed

In minutes, the rocket escaped gravity's grip. The Atlas booster slipped away. John was making history! His first orbit took place without a problem. At superfast speed, John saw both sunrise and sunset from his window.

John Glenn in *Friendship 7* as it orbits Earth.

It took John 90 minutes to complete an orbit.

John said he was flying through "yellowish green" dots. The dots glowed like "fireflies on a real dark night."

On Earth, John's words startled the crew in the control center. Their surprise quickly gave way to alarm. John's capsule flashed a frightening signal on the center's control panel. *Friendship 7*'s landing bag and heat shield had come loose.

The crew in the control room follows John's flight.

3,000° F

The heat shield was critical. Without it, John's capsule would not be safe from the blistering heat of **reentry**. If *Friendship 7* burned up, John would die.

Mercury heat shield

The heat shield protected the capsule from scorching heat when it returned to Earth's atmosphere.

Anxiously, the crew in the control center worked to get John safely home. They suggested that he leave the **retropack** on the capsule to keep the heat shield in place. The retropack was usually dropped before reentry. Would it survive the 3,000° F (1,649° C) temperatures the capsule faced?

The next moments were nerve-racking. Reentry's scorching heat blocked radio signals. At Mission Control, no one could communicate with John.

The retropack, made up of three rockets, was attached to the capsule with metal straps.

"That Was a Real Fireball, Boy"

In the capsule, John watched pieces of metal and fiery "chunks" fly past the window. John wondered if they were from the heat shield.

At the control center, everyone waited nervously. Alan Shepard called to John. "Do you receive? Over." There was no answer. The ground crew feared John had burned up like a **meteor**.

Alan B. Shepard tensely follows John Glenn's progress.

The heat shield on John's capsule had never really come loose. The signal received on Earth was faulty.

Shepard called again and again. "Do you receive? Over."

"Loud and clear," John finally said. His voice filled everyone with great relief. "That was a real fireball, boy."

Through the blaze of reentry, John Glenn survived his superfast flight. He soon parachuted safely back to Earth.

The first American to orbit Earth, John Glenn was greeted with a ticker-tape parade in New York City.

Changing Goals, Changing Rockets

As goals for space travel changed, so did the rockets. The Apollo moon **missions** needed special spacecrafts. Apollo rockets had three parts, called modules. The service module held the engine. The command module carried the crew. The lunar module landed on the moon.

The largest rocket ever built, Saturn V heaved *Apollo 11* into space. It could travel up to 25,000 miles per hour (40,234 kph).

Astronaut Edwin E. "Buzz" Aldrin, Jr., walks on the moon, July 20, 1969, with lunar module in background.

Before 1981, rockets were not **reusable**. That changed with the space shuttle *Columbia*. Shuttles blast off like rockets and land like gliders. Two of their parts can be used again, so flights can take place more often.

In 2001, the *Odyssey* **space probe** began to orbit Mars. *Odyssey* could pave the way for **manned** Mars flights. History may be made yet again!

Odyssey has sent stunning images of dusty red Mars back to Earth. Where is the spacecraft now? Check mars.jpl.nasa.gov/odyssey/mission/rightnow.html to find out!

JUST THE FACTS   More About Rockets and Space

- Early rockets couldn't lift heavy spacecrafts, so *Friendship 7* and other early crafts were small and lightweight.

- NASA's Goddard Space Flight Center was named for Robert Goddard.

- The powerful Saturn V rockets were 363 feet (111 m) tall.

- To leave the moon, the lunar module broke in two. Its bottom became a launch pad to lift the top part into space.

TIMELINE   This timeline shows some important events in the history of rockets and spaceflight.

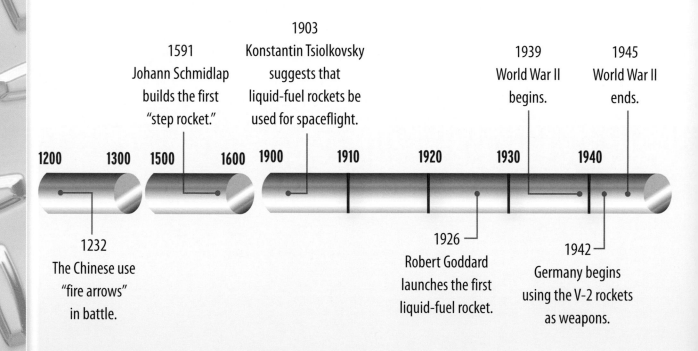

1903
Konstantin Tsiolkovsky suggests that liquid-fuel rockets be used for spaceflight.

1591
Johann Schmidlap builds the first "step rocket."

1939
World War II begins.

1945
World War II ends.

1200   1300   1500   1600   1900   1910   1920   1930   1940

1232
The Chinese use "fire arrows" in battle.

1926
Robert Goddard launches the first liquid-fuel rocket.

1942
Germany begins using the V-2 rockets as weapons.

- Space shuttles are launched to the east. That way, Earth's rotation can give them an extra boost.

- Space shuttles have been used to dock to space stations, take satellites into orbit, and make space repairs.

In 1998, John Glenn made history once more. At 77 years old, he became the oldest person in space.

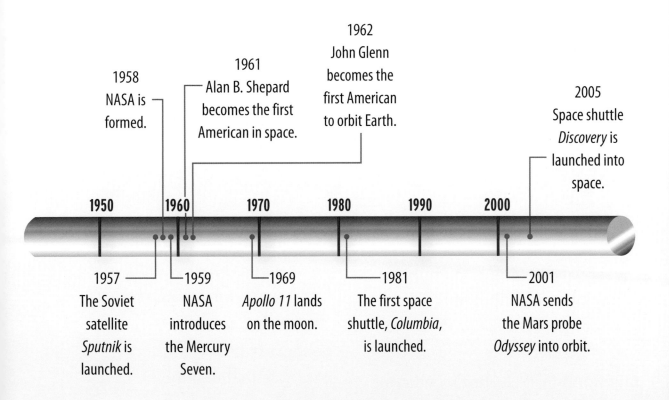

1958
NASA is
formed.

1961
Alan B. Shepard
becomes the first
American in space.

1962
John Glenn
becomes the
first American
to orbit Earth.

2005
Space shuttle
Discovery is
launched into
space.

1950   1960   1970   1980   1990   2000

1957
The Soviet
satellite
Sputnik is
launched.

1959
NASA
introduces
the Mercury
Seven.

1969
Apollo 11 lands
on the moon.

1981
The first space
shuttle, *Columbia*,
is launched.

2001
NASA sends
the Mars probe
Odyssey into orbit.

GLOSSARY

atmosphere (AT-muhss-fihr) the mixture of gases surrounding Earth

capsule (KAP-suhl) the part of a rocket that holds the crew

cosmonaut (KOZ-muh-nawt) a Russian astronaut

fuel (FYOO-uhl) something that supplies power when burned

Godspeed (god-SPEED) an expression used to wish someone safe travels or success

gravity (GRAV-uh-tee) the force that pulls things toward Earth, the sun, or other bodies in space

hatch (HACH) a covered hole in a door

manned (MAND) supplied with people

meteor (MEE-tee-ur) a chunk of rock or metal that falls from space and burns up in Earth's atmosphere

missions (MISH-uhnz) certain jobs to be performed in space

orbit (OR-bit) to travel around a planet, the sun, or other object

oxygen (OK-suh-juhn) a colorless, odorless gas in the air, which people breathe

reentry (ree-EN-tree) returning to Earth's atmostphere

retropack (RET-roh-pak) a group of rockets on a spacecraft, used for slowing or changing direction

reusable (ree-YOO-zuh-buhl) something that can be used again

satellite (SAT-uh-lite) a spacecraft that is placed in orbit

soared (SORD) flew or rose very high into the air

space probe (SPAYSS PROHB) a spacecraft that studies space and sends information back to Earth

spacecraft (SPAYSS-kraft) a vehicle that can travel in space

BIBLIOGRAPHY

Chaikin, Andrew. *Space: A History of Space Exploration in Photographs.* Buffalo, NY: Firefly Books (2002).

Glover, Linda K. *National Geographic Encyclopedia of Space.* Washington, D.C.: National Geographic (2004).

Kranz, Gene. *Failure Is Not an Option: Mission Control From Mercury to Apollo 13 and Beyond.* New York: Simon & Schuster (2000).

NASA. *"A Brief History of Rocketry."* quest.arc.nasa.gov/space/teachers/rockets/history.html

Reichhardt, Tony, ed. *Space Shuttle: The First Twenty Years—Astronauts' Experiences in Their Own Words.* New York: DK Publishing (2002).

READ MORE

Cole, Michael D. *NASA Space Vehicles: Capsules, Shuttles, and Space Stations.* Berkley Heights, NJ: Enslow (2000).

Farndon, John. *Rockets and Other Spacecraft (How Science Works).* Brookfield, CT: Copper Beech Books (2000).

Hawkes, Nigel. *The Fantastic Cutaway Book of Spacecraft.* Brookfield, CT: Copper Beech Books (1995).

Miller, Ron. *The History of Rockets.* New York: Franklin Watts (1998).

LEARN MORE ONLINE

Visit these Web sites to learn more about rockets and their history:

liftoff.msfc.nasa.gov/academy/rocket_sci/rocket_sci.html

www.nasm.si.edu/

www.spaceflight.nasa.gov/home/index.html

INDEX

ABOUT THE AUTHOR

Donna Latham is a writer in the Chicago, Illinois, area. One of her favorite childhood memories is of watching the *Apollo 11* moon landing on TV.